SELF

Even Me

BRITTANY JOY

30 DAY JOURNAL

Publishing company:
KDP publishing

Publisher:
Self-published by Brittany Joy

Graphic Designer:
Created by Author with Canva

Editor:
Alysha Diane
The Sophisticated EntrepreneuHER

Photographer:
@romeomadeit on Instagram

ISBN-978-0-578-87638-2

Dedications

I want to dedicate this journal to the people in my life that have pushed me listen, learn, understand, and teach.

My Grandparents:
Although you are not physically here with me, I carry your spirit.

My Parents:
Mom, I watched you bury my dad and both of your parents. I can't express how your strength has molded me to be strong and Walk with my head held high. To my dad, thank you for teaching me stand up for myself.

My Son:
Ethan, you are my biggest hero! You tell me every day I make you proud and you will never know the magnitude of that.

My Crew:
Charlie, Kimiasheia, and Shirah, thank you for being my knees when I couldn't stand and lending your heart when I felt mine was broken.

My Amazing Mentors:
Lori Jennings, Dr. Tonja Williams, Dr. Lendozia Edwards, Donna Lamb, Dr. Jewel Brazelton, Tamera French and Paula Farmer, I can never repay you for the time and love you have poured into me. Thank you for being the logic and the love I needed when I could not be those things for myself.

Last but certainly not least a special thank you to my editor, Alysha Diane, for supporting me through this project and being an amazing teammate.

I love and appreciate each of you immensely!!

To my readers, I hope this will help you become the best you. Live to learn and learn to love. Life is not full of failures; it is full of lessons.

Let your Self Care Journey begin!

Today's word is....

EMPOWERED

How will I incorporate today's word?

What does today's word mean to you?

Your thoughts for today...

Today's word is....

RESILIENT

How will I incorporate today's word?

What does today's word mean to you?

Your thoughts for today...

Today's word is....

CONFIDENT

How will I incorporate today's word?

What does today's word mean to you?

Your thoughts for today...

Today's word is....

FOCUS

How will I incorporate today's word?

What does today's word mean to you?

Your thoughts for today...

Today's word is....

KIND

How will I incorporate today's word?

What does today's word mean to you?

Your thoughts for today...

Today's word is....

DECISIVE

How will I incorporate today's word?

What does today's word mean to you?

Your thoughts for today...

Today's word is....

CALM

How will I incorporate today's word?

What does today's word mean to you?

Your thoughts for today...

Today's word is....

BOLD

How will I incorporate today's word?

What does today's word mean to you?

Your thoughts for today...

Today's word is....

WILLING

How will I incorporate today's word?

What does today's word mean to you?

Your thoughts for today...

Today's word is....

STRONG

How will I incorporate today's word?

What does today's word mean to you?

Your thoughts for today...

Today's word is....

INSPIRE

How will I incorporate today's word?

What does today's word mean to you?

Your thoughts for today...

Today is_____

Today's word is....

BRAVE

How will I incorporate today's word?

What does today's word mean to you?

Your thoughts for today...

Today's word is....

FREEDOM

How will I incorporate today's word?

What does today's word mean to you?

Your thoughts for today...

Today's word is....

CLEAR

How will I incorporate today's word?

What does today's word mean to you?

Your thoughts for today...

Today's word is....

OPEN

How will I incorporate today's word?

What does today's word mean to you?

Your thoughts for today...

Today's word is....

ACCEPTANCE

How will I incorporate today's word?

What does today's word mean to you?

Your thoughts for today...

Today's word is....

GRATEFUL

How will I incorporate today's word?

What does today's word mean to you?

Your thoughts for today...

Today's word is....

WISDOM

How will I incorporate today's word?

What does today's word mean to you?

Your thoughts for today...

Today's word is....

COURAGEOUS

How will I incorporate today's word?

What does today's word mean to you?

Your thoughts for today...

Today's word is....

HEALED

How will I incorporate today's word?

What does today's word mean to you?

Your thoughts for today...

Today's word is....

VALUE

How will I incorporate today's word?

What does today's word mean to you?

Your thoughts for today...

Today's word is....

SUCCESS

How will I incorporate today's word?

What does today's word mean to you?

Your thoughts for today...

Today's word is....

AWARE

How will I incorporate today's word?

What does today's word mean to you?

Your thoughts for today...

Today's word is....

SINCERE

How will I incorporate today's word?

What does today's word mean to you?

Your thoughts for today...

Today's word is....

THOUGHTFUL

How will I incorporate today's word?

What does today's word mean to you?

Your thoughts for today...

Today's word is....

PEACEFUL

How will I incorporate today's word?

What does today's word mean to you?

Your thoughts for today...

Today's word is....

GENUINE

How will I incorporate today's word?

What does today's word mean to you?

Your thoughts for today...

Today is_____

Today's word is....

HELPFUL

How will I incorporate today's word?

What does today's word mean to you?

Your thoughts for today...

Today is_____

Today's word is....

LEADER

How will I incorporate today's word?

What does today's word mean to you?

Your thoughts for today...

Today's word is....

POSITIVE

How will I incorporate today's word?

What does today's word mean to you?

Your thoughts for today...

Made in the USA
Monee, IL
18 June 2021